# The Snopp on the Sidewalk

### and Other Poems

by JACK PRELUTSKY

pictures by BYRON BARTON

With love to Wendy C. who showed the Snopp to me

**GREENWILLOW BOOKS**
A DIVISION OF WILLIAM MORROW & COMPANY, INC., NEW YORK

Text copyright © 1976, 1977 by Jack Prelutsky.    Illustrations copyright © 1977 by Byron Barton.    All rights reserved. No part of this book may be reproduced without permission from Greenwillow Books, 105 Madison Ave., N.Y. 10016. Printed in U.S.A.    1  2  3  4  5
Library of Congress Cataloging in Publication Data    Prelutsky, Jack.   The snopp on the sidewalk, and other poems.    I.   Nonsense-verses.
[1.   Nonsense verses]   I.   Barton, Byron.   II.   Title.   PZ8.3.P9Sn   811'.5'4   76-46323   ISBN 0-688-80084-X   ISBN 0-688-84084-1 lib. bdg.

## THE SNOPP
## ON THE SIDEWALK

It was lying on the sidewalk
like a gray old ragged mop,
but the second that I saw it,
I was sure I'd found the snopp.

It did not move a fiber
of its long and shaggy hair,
as if seeming not to notice
that I stood and watched it there.

At first I thought, "I'll touch it,"
and then I thought, "I won't,"
but when again I thought, "I will,"
the snopp said softly, "Don't."

This startled me so greatly
that I turned to run away,
but as I started down the street,
the snopp called after, "Stay."

I asked, "What do you want of me,
for snopp, I cannot guess?"
The snopp, still never stirring,
only answered me with, "Yes."

I did not understand this
so I tried once more to go,
but I'd barely started homeward
when the snopp said sweetly, "No."

And so I stayed that day and night,
and yes, I stayed a week,
and nevermore in all that time
did either of us speak.

At last I said, "Oh snopp, dear snopp,
I really have to go."
The snopp showed no emotion
as it whispered only, "Oh."

I headed home, not looking back,
afraid to ever stop.
I knew that if I paused but once
I'd never leave the snopp.

But the snopp remains within my mind,
I'm sure it always will—
that strange thing on the sidewalk
that I'm certain lies there still.

## THE GIBBLE

The gibble is glum and big as a thumb,
it lives in the deep green grasses
and looks around with an angry frown
at everyone who passes.

But should you roam about his home,
you need not fear the gibble;
it's much too small to gobble you all
(though it just might take a nibble).

# THE MONUMENTAL MEATH

I had skipped across the meadow
and was hopping through the heath
when I stepped into the shadow
of the monumental meath.

It towered far above me
as I cowered underneath
and I feared I'd soon be eaten
by the monumental meath.

But it bowed and whispered softly,
oh so softly spoke the meath,
as it sadly said, "Fear nothing,
you are free to leave the heath

for alack, I cannot eat you,"
(here a moan escaped the meath)
then it sighed "Alas" and left me.
I was spared! . . . It had no teeth.

## WRIMPLES

When the clock strikes five but it's only four,
there's a wrimple in your clock.
When your key won't work in your own front door,
there's a wrimple in the lock.

When your brand-new shoes refuse to fit,
there's a wrimple in each shoe.
When the lights go out and they just were lit,
that's a wrimple's doing too.

When you shake and shake but the salt won't pour,
there's a wrimple in the salt.
When your cake falls flat on the kitchen floor,
it's surely a wrimple's fault.

The way to fix these irksome works
is obvious and simple.
Just search and find it where it lurks,
and then . . . remove the wrimple.

## THE WOZZIT

There's a wozzit in the closet
and it's making quite a mess.
It has eaten father's trousers,
it has eaten mother's dress,
and it's making so much noise
as it gobbles down my toys,
there's a wozzit in the closet—
oh I'm certain . . . yes, oh yes!

There's a wozzit in the closet
and I don't know what to do.
It has swallowed sister's slippers,
it has chewed upon my shoe,
now it's having its dessert
for it's stuffing down my shirt,
there's a wozzit in the closet—
yes, oh yes, I know it's true!

And I also know I'll never never
open up that closet,
for I never never never
ever
want to meet that wozzit.

## HELP!

Can anybody tell me, please,
a bit about the thing
with seven legs and furry knees,
four noses and a wing?

Oh what has prickles on its chin,
what's yellow, green and blue,
and what has soft and slimy skin?
Oh tell me, tell me, do.

And tell me, what has polka dots
on every other ear,
what ties its tail in twenty knots,
what weeps a purple tear?

Oh what is growling long and low
and please, has it been fed?
I think I'd really better know . . .
it's sitting on my head.

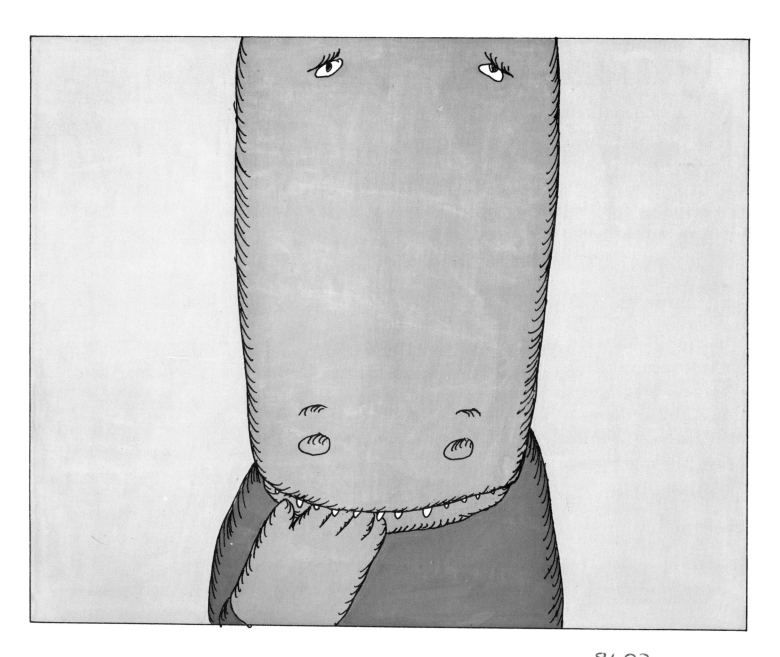

# THE GROBBLES

The grobbles are gruesome
the grobbles are green
the grobbles are nasty
the grobbles are mean
the grobbles hide deep
in a hollowy tree
just waiting to gobble
whomever they see.

I walk through the woods
for I'm quite unaware
that the grobbles are waiting
to gobble me there
they suddenly spring
from their hollowy tree
oh goodness! the grobbles
are gobbling m. . . .

## FLONSTER POEM

The flime devoured the floober
and the flummie dined on flime,
the fleemie gulped the flummie down
in scarcely any time.

The fleener chewed the fleemie,
but in hardly half a wink
he was swallowed by the floodoo,
who was eaten by the flink.

The flink was rather careless
and was gobbled to the bone
by an enterprising flibble,
who fell victim to the flone.

The floath who fed upon the flone
soon met another floath,
and while they wondered what to do . . .

THE FLAKKER ATE THEM BOTH!

## IT

I lie in my bed, trying hard to sleep,
but I hear it crawl and I hear it creep.
It starts and it stops, then it stays quite still,
and it makes me feel a chill.

Oh I know it is there, for it moves around,
it makes a soft but definite sound,
and I don't know what it could possibly be,
but I hope that it won't find me.

Oh I hear it there as it nears my bed,
and my teeth are chattering in my head,
for I hear it nibble and I hear it chew,
oh what does it want to do?

It is there, it is there, it is surely there,
though I don't know why or exactly where,
what it wants it will not say,
but I wish it would go away.

## SPLATT!

The blatt, though flat, was also fat.
The snatt, not flat, was fatter.
that fatter snatt sat on the blatt,
and now the blatt's still flatter.

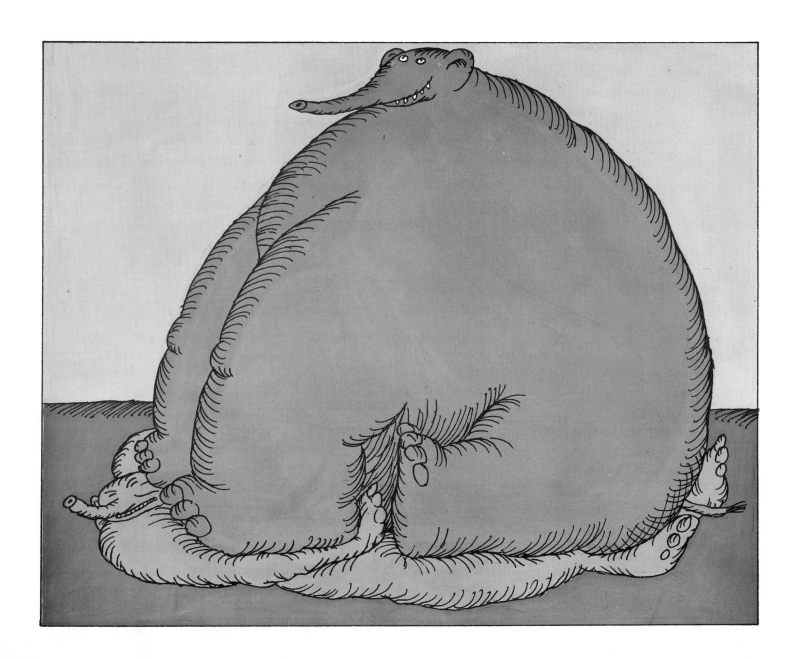

## THE LURPP IS ON THE LOOSE

Oh the lurpp is on the loose, the loose,
the lurpp is on the loose.
It caused a fretful, frightful fuss
when it swallowed a ship and ate a bus,
and now it's after all of us,
oh the lurpp is on the loose.

Oh the lurpp is on the loose, the loose,
the lurpp is on the loose.
It weighs about a zillion pounds,
it's making loud and lurppy sounds
as it follows us with bumbly bounds,
oh the lurpp is on the loose.

Oh the lurpp is on the loose, the loose,
the lurpp is on the loose.
It's covered with horns and thorns and claws
and razor teeth adorn its jaws,
so everyone's running away, because
the lurpp is on the loose.

# THE FRUMMICK AND THE FRELLY

The frummick and the frelly
sat beneath a silver sky,
spreading jingleberry jelly
over pinkadoodle pie.

The frelly weighed a hundred tons,
the frummick matched its size.
They both ate bales of boiling buns
and countless piles of pies.

The frelly and the frummick
were in fairly mellow moods
as they stuffed their massive stomachs
with a great array of foods.

They fared on pairs of pickled yare
and shared a score of sneel.
They gorged on gare both burnt and rare
in their exotic meal.

They ate a clutch of candied snutch
and troves of tasty troove
in such a way they ate so much
that they could barely move.

And in that way, for quite some while,
the weighty couple sat,
each seeming, in its special style,
contented, full and fat.

"There's nothing left to eat, dear friend,"
the frelly said at last.
"I fear our feast is at an end,
and such a fine repast."

"Ah fine, so fine," the frummick sighed
and scratched its bulging belly,
then opened wide and stuffed inside
the flabbergasted frelly.